HEART
TALK

HEART TALK

POETIC WISDOM FOR A BETTER LIFE

(handwritten: A BETTER inserted before LIFE)

CLEO WADE

37INK

—

ATRIA

New York ❤ London ❤ Toronto ❤ Sydney ❤ New Delhi

37INK

ATRIA

An Imprint of Simon & Schuster, Inc.
1230 Avenue of the Americas
New York, NY 10020

First 37INK/Atria Paperback Canadian export edition February 2018

37INK / ATRIA PAPERBACK and colophon are trademarks of
Simon & Schuster, Inc.

For information about special discounts for bulk purchases, please
contact Simon & Schuster Special Sales at 1-866-506-1949 or
business@simonandschuster.com.

The Simon & Schuster Speakers Bureau can bring authors to your
live event. For more information or to book an event, contact the
Simon & Schuster Speakers Bureau at 1-866-248-3049 or visit
our website at www.simonspeakers.com.

Interior design by Laura Palese

Manufactured in the United States of America

10 9 8 7 6 5 4 3 2 1

Library of Congress Cataloging-in-Publication Data is available.

ISBN 978-1-5011-9769-7
ISBN 978-1-5011-7735-4 (ebook)

This is dedicated
to every human being
who looks different, feels different,
and thinks differently.
I see you. I feel you. I am you.
Stay different. Our world needs
the difference we will make.

Dearest You,

I have experienced just about every type of heartbreak that exists. The kind that happens with a romantic partner, with someone I wished were a romantic partner, with a family member, a friend, even a stranger. I've known the heartbreak associated with professional situations and things I aspire to: a dream that never came true, or a dream that did come true, but when it did, it wasn't meant to be. I have even broken my own heart a few times (more than a few, actually).

What I have learned from having my heart in pieces is that our stories are important. They help us take our pieces and build something new. And if we build with love they can help us build something even better than we had before.

When we get real and honest and raw about what we go through, we have the power to turn our words into medicine and our experiences into wisdom.

This book is a compilation of notes I have written in my apartment in New York City. It also consists of poems about loving, being, and healing that have been my life rafts when I did not know how to swim in the waters of the world. You will also find the type of good ol'-fashioned heartfelt advice I would share with you if we were sitting in my home at my kitchen table (by the way, thanks, Mom, for showing me the healing power of kitchen-table conversation).

I hope that in reading this book you will be reminded of your strength, reintroduced to your resilience, and reconnected with your personal power and love of self.

And if you would like to treat this book less like a book and more like a friend or a companion, I would like that very much.

Also, you should know that I love you. I don't need to know you to love you. If this pile of papers found its way into your life, it is because we are meant to be. You are my tribe, and I am yours.

If you have any questions, complaints, new ideas, love notes, or invitations for tea, I am here for you, talk to me: HeartTalk@cleowade.com.

Love,
Cleo

PS: Along the way, you will find that I have written some notes in the margins throughout this book. I did this in hopes that you'll feel welcomed to not treat this book too preciously. Write in it, rip out a page and pin it on the fridge, read it front to back, or pick a page to read at random when you need a moment to yourself to recharge. Let these words show up for you however you'd like. No rules.

HEART
TALK

GET HONEST WITH YOURSELF.
BE THE PERSON YOU
ARE THE CLEAREST WITH.

BE THE PERSON YOU ARE
THE MOST FEARLESS WITH.

THESE ARE THE SEEDS
THAT TURN YOUR LIFE
INTO A GARDEN OF
AUTHENTICITY.

FIRST THINGS FIRST:

SELF - CARE.

Self-care is how we fuel our self-love so that we are able to share our love with everyone around us. Our hearts are warm when we are able to show up with generosity, patience, and compassion for the ones we love, but we must remember that it is impossible to truly be there for others without taking care of ourselves first. We take care of ourselves by asking what our needs are. We take care of ourselves by making healthy choices when it comes to our physical and emotional bodies. We take care of ourselves by lightening up and not being so damn hard on ourselves. At times, life seems to be one never-ending to-do list, but we must learn to disrupt the flood of life's demands in order to replenish our energy so that we can fully show up for all of our passions and responsibilities. It does not benefit anyone when we live our lives running on fumes. Love is an action, a thing in motion. Therefore, it requires fuel.

ONLY A FULL TANK CAN GO THE DISTANCE.

hiding and seeking

when I let go
of who
I thought I had to be
I could
finally
and powerfully
become who
I really am
oh,
to find out
I had been hiding
and did not know that
(self-)love
had been looking
for me
all along

cleo wade

YOU WANT TO

FIND LOVE?

LOSE YOUR FEAR.

YOU WANT TO

STAY IN LOVE?

LOSE YOUR EGO.

How many times have we let our fear of getting hurt or disappointed keep us from love? Love requires us to unpack our fear and pain so those feelings do not interfere with our ability to thrive in connection with others. This process requires a level of bravery, vulnerability, and intimacy that can be scary and deeply uncomfortable, but real love only exists outside of our comfort zone. We can only step into love when we leave our fear behind. To be fearless is to be afraid of something but to do it anyway. Be fearless. Take the first step. Once we choose love, the work to maintain our love begins. The first step in this is conquering our ego. A loving relationship is built on compromise and working with our part-ner to continuously evolve into our best selves. This is not possible without hard truths, tough conver-sations, personal growth, and behavioral shifts. The ego does not like any of this. The ego wants us to believe that we are always right and that our way of doing things is always the best way. Our spirit, on the other hand, knows that the people we love are in our life to challenge us to rise to new levels of consideration and care in all that we do. We cannot truly choose to invest in love while our ego is pres-ent, for real love runs on *selflessness*, and the ego runs on *selfishness*. ❦

AND THE BEST NEWS
OF ALL IS THAT IT IS
NEVER TOO LATE TO
BECOME THE PERSON
YOU'VE ALWAYS
WANTED TO BE.

cleo wade

Take a deep breath and go for it. Don't allow the energy of procrastination to create a staleness surrounding your dreams. Breath is a sign of the body living. When you inhale deeply, you are reminded that you are alive and that every moment represents a new possibility for you to step into your destiny.

DON'T BE THE ONE YOU ARE WAITING ON.

it's only natural

of course
I've changed,
darling . . .
I've grown.

Change is necessary. It is important. And it is also what makes life exciting. When we fear change, it keeps us in an energy of feeling stuck, powerless, and resentful, but when we embrace change, we open ourselves to the understanding that anything is possible. Life is not supposed to stay the same. We are not supposed to stay the same. Our life, our communities, and our world are always in bloom. When we understand this, we see that change is growth, and growth is essential for each of us to reach our individual and collective potential. ❧

all of it

which parts of yourself won't you let yourself
love yet?

befriend your ingredients

the spicy, the sweet, the pain, the heartache, the gifts, the shame,
and the shine

fall
in love
with
all
of you

savor
yourself

FOUR STEPS FOR OPENING YOURSELF
UP TO A MORE RADICAL LIFE:

1. LOVE YOURSELF ENOUGH TO GET
   TO KNOW YOURSELF.

2. ACHIEVE STEP ONE BY HAVING
   THE COURAGE TO ASK YOURSELF
   THE HARD QUESTIONS.

3. HONOR STEP TWO BY HAVING
   THE COURAGE TO ANSWER THE
   HARD QUESTIONS.

4. REPEAT STEPS 1-3 YOUR
   WHOLE LIFE.

heart talk

KNOWING YOUR NEEDS
IS A SUPERPOWER.

Our world often tells us that there is something wrong with needing something or someone, or that expressing our needs is somehow a sign of weakness. This is completely untrue. Knowing our needs is a limitless superpower, one that can help us make all the big decisions in life. When we know what we need from a partner, we spend much less time dating the wrong people. When we know what we need to feel challenged and motivated by our work, we are much more tuned in to what we want our career path to look like. And when we know what we need in order to be our best selves, we are much better at showing up as that person in our relationships with our friends and family. Be unapologetic when it comes to your needs. They are, at the very least, deserving of being seen and heard. What are your needs? Create a list of your needs and make space for them in your life. Respecting and expressing your needs can superpower your life. Start by recognizing them. ❧

WE MAY NOT ALWAYS HAVE THE
POWER TO CONTROL WHAT SHOWS
UP AT OUR DOOR, BUT WE
ALWAYS, ALWAYS, ALWAYS HAVE THE
POWER TO DECIDE WHAT STAYS
AND WHAT GOES.

No matter how much work we do on ourselves, stress and anxiety will still show up. Our work is not to avoid them; it isn't to wrestle with them or "cope" with them. Stress and anxiety are unavoidable visitors. Let us accept this. When they come, acknowledge their arrival, evaluate what invited them in, and recognize that they are guests, not permanent fixtures. They will leave, especially if we don't entertain them or pick a fight with them. No matter how overwhelming the feelings that come with stress and anxiety are, we must always remember that we are human, and though we may not be able to control their arrival, we always have the power to release them. Pause. Breathe slowly and deliberately. Think positively. Remember your strength. These feelings will eventually leave, because ultimately they know they have no home within your sacred self. ❦

YES? YES. YES!

We spend so much of our lives hearing others tell us to go after what we want, but few speak to the anxiety that often comes once we actually get what we want. We cannot have our dreams if we do not learn to say yes to them. Achieving our goals and desires is only as powerful as our ability to receive them. We are all familiar with the act of standing in our own way. Sometimes it is because we are scared: You are in the final interview of your dream job and all of a sudden you start thinking, "Can I really do this?" Or you finally meet the romantic partner that you know you deserve and then ask yourself, "Am I worthy?" Yes. You can do it. Yes. You are worthy. Move out of your own way and say yes to yourself and yes to the world. Say yes. In fact, don't just say yes . . . celebrate your yes. It is a victory. ⚘

it was time

so I said yes
I said yes to living
I said yes to loving
I said yes to being
my . . .
self
illuminated
and unafraid

cleo wade

LET GO OF SHAME.

IT WILL NOT ADD

A SINGLE SMILE,

DOLLAR, OR MINUTE

TO YOUR LIFE.

love never lies

shame never tells
the truth
it tells you
you are not
good enough
the truth is
you are
it tells you
you have to be perfect
the truth is
you don't
it tells you
your mistakes
are fatal wounds
the truth is
you heal
it tells you
everything has fallen apart
the truth is
you will rebuild
it tells you
that you will stay sunken in despair
the truth is
you will rise

cleo wade

it tells you
you failed
you lost
& you got hurt
the truth is
you learned (what to do next time)
you gained (knowledge from your
knockdown)
& you found out (just how strong you
are)
it says
you will never make it
the truth is
keep going
for
shame said
you would never
survive
and the truth is
you
are
still
here

NOT EVERY
GROUND
IS A
BATTLE-
GROUND

Wise soldiers know that not every ground is a battleground. Their scars do not let them forget that they have had to be a fighter, but their scars also do not let them forget that the human body cannot live every day in the trenches. To exist in a state that requires you to constantly be prepared to go to war is exhausting. No human body or soul can sustain that type of energy as a lifestyle. Let yourself relax. The ground is not only the place where we march toward what we must fight for; it is also a place where we are being divinely held up by the earth. 🌱

GRATITUDE IS A SPIRITUAL

AND ECONOMICAL

FORM OF STRESS RELIEF.

cleo wade

Learning the power of gratitude is not only wise, it is practical. When we understand how to feel grateful for what we have, we are free from the uneasy state of constantly wanting. A never-ending hunt for more puts the mind in a continual state of anxiety. But when we are thankful for what we have and understand the difference between what we want and what we need, we are able to relax the mind and put less pressure on ourselves to obsessively upgrade the things in our life. Release the energy of more, more, more and replace it with the energy of thank you, thank you, thank you. ❧

IF YOU AREN'T STAYING IN THE MOMENT, YOU ARE LEAVING IT.

My brother once said to me, "If you are not staying present in the moment, you are leaving it." Those words really struck me. They made me realize that if I did not develop a practice of staying present, I would spend my entire life leaving wherever I was. The only way we can make the most of our lives is to make the most of our moments. Today, wherever you are, decide to stay. We can know the gifts that lie in the present only if we stay in it long enough to receive them. ❦

SOMETIMES THE BEST PRESENT IS BEING PRESENT.

IF YOU WANT TO FEEL EMPOWERED

BY ALL OF YOUR DECISIONS, YOU

CAN'T JUST CALCULATE YOUR RISKS.

YOU HAVE TO FULLY AND TOTALLY

ACCEPT YOUR RISKS AS WELL. ◄─────

cleo wade

When we apply the energy of acceptance to risk-taking, we are able to take risks with much more confidence and steadiness. Acceptance is when we bring trust to a situation. We all take risks, but if we want to master risk-taking, we must learn to do so without attaching anxious energy to our decisions. Anxiety disconnects us from our power. Acceptance allows us to relax into our power and move through any circumstance with clarity and confidence. ❦

TAKE RISKS WITH FAITH, NOT FEAR.

MAY ALL OF
YOUR VIBES SAY:

I GOT THIS.

Confidence is not something we have, it is something we practice so that it lives in flow with all that we do. Confidence is not something we have by saying "Okay, I need to be confident right now." True confidence comes from affirming ourselves regularly and treating ourselves kindly. When our mental chatter props us up and reminds us that we are capable of whatever we wish to accomplish, half of the battle of achieving any goal is already won. Don't approach your life from a space of defeat. Approach your life with the vibrancy of "I got this," because at the end of the day . . . who is to say you don't?

cleo wade

When we live with honesty, positive intentions, fairness, love, integrity, and transparency, we do not need to spend our time explaining ourselves to others. Explanations are necessary only when our actions require justifications, and justifications are necessary only when our intentions are murky. Live your life with clear and good intentions and you will never have to spend your time explaining what you do or who you are. ❧

I choose to shine

what is within us
appears before us
when I
think like
a cactus too long
I am all of a sudden
a cactus
I am in the desert
I am without water
and not even
the one I love
can
touch me
so I think
like the sun instead
and
nourish
the growth of
all
with my
light
and my
warmth

cleo wade

CLEAN OUT YOUR THOUGHTS —

THEY HAVE THE POWER TO COVER

YOUR ENTIRE LIFE IN DIRT.

Healthy thinking is when we choose to guide our thoughts in a way that benefits our best self. Every thought, especially our repetitive thoughts, manifests itself in our lives. For example, if we are stuck in a thought cycle of "I am not good enough," we will start to see the outside world affirm that thought. We may also find our behavior begin to affirm that thought when we isolate ourselves from the people in our lives who love us and know that we are good enough. Since our thoughts are what frame our lives, the first step to constructing a healthy life is to construct healthy thoughts. Healthy thinking does not mean you never have dark thoughts; it just means that you don't stay in unhelpful thoughts long enough for them to influence your reality. We become the stories we tell ourselves, so it is crucial that we, as narrators, frame our experiences with thoughts that heal, nurture, and motivate us. We are more in charge of our thoughts than we think. Keep your inner world loving and hopeful, and your outside world will begin to reflect exactly that. ❦

LOVE YOUR-SELF ENOUGH

Love yourself enough to walk into only the rooms and situations that show care and love for you. Love yourself enough to walk out of the rooms that harm you in any way. Love yourself enough to hold the people who harm you accountable for their words and actions. Love yourself enough to express your wants, your needs, and your desires. Love yourself enough to tell the truth. Love yourself enough to keep yourself safe. Love yourself enough to say enough is enough when enough has become enough. ❥

A LOVE LIKE THIS MOVES MOUNTAINS.

be heard

sing your song

if that is what
is inside of you
sing
your
damn
song

do
your soul
that
favor

You are the only person who truly decides who you are. If you want to be a singer . . . think like a singer, say you are a singer, and of course sing your song. We spend so much of our lives waiting for others to qualify us. Authorize *yourself.* Step into your power right now; give yourself your own credentials, and *you* be the one who qualifies who you are. Why not? Nobody knows you better than you do. ❧

BE KIND.

IT SHAKES THE WORLD.

There is no way to give kindness to another without knowing it in ourselves first. We must continually ask ourselves (especially on our tough days when we are feeling the most hurt or irritated): Is this the kindest thought I could have? Is this the kindest thing I could say? Is this the kindest action I could take in this situation? To achieve a kinder world, we must approach kindness with ambition and dedication. We must practice it in every moment of our lives. Kindness is that important. ❧

JUST A FRIENDLY REMINDER:
NOTHING ABOUT YOU IS A MISTAKE.
YOU ARE A GIFT AND YOU ARE HERE
FOR A REASON. YOU DESERVE
TO TAKE UP SPACE IN THE
WORLD, AND WE NEED YOU HERE.

cleo wade

stand tall

the tree never
feels less like a tree
because it is different
from the others
in the forest

so why would *we* ever think we are meant to all be the same?

to be unique is to be a living thing

KNOW THE VALUE OF KNOWING YOUR VALUE.

Some of the best advice I ever received was when my first mentor at my first real job in New York City told me, "Don't wait on anyone to tell you what you are worth. You have to be the first person who knows what you are worth and can say what you are worth." I have always kept that advice close to me when navigating the waters of not only my work but also my personal relationships. In the world of work, you have to be the first one who knows the value of your talents and also the first one who can express what you are worth to your boss, client, or collaborator. Similarly, in the world of dating and relationships, you have to be the first one to tell another person how your time and energy deserve to be treated. When we know our value and can express our value, we are able to teach others how to honor what we bring to the table. ❦

WHAT WE DO AND HOW WE SPEAK
IS EITHER CONSTRUCTIVE OR
DESTRUCTIVE. CHOOSE TO BE
CONSTRUCTIVE. DON'T BE A
BULLDOZER WHERE LIFE CALLS
ON YOU TO BE A BUILDER.

cleo wade

Very few decisions in life leave us in a neutral space. Most of the decisions we make when it comes to work, family, and relationships are either constructive or destructive. Ask yourself: Which are you choosing? Is the way you treat your loved one building your bond or breaking it apart? Does your behavior toward them chip away at your trust or solidify it? How are you treating yourself? The body, mind, and spirit require constructive thoughts and actions in order to build your best possible life. Don't tear yourself down when you have the power to build yourself up. ❦

I did not lose the lesson

I did a lot of things
not in the right way
some may even call them
mistakes

I just call them
the scars
that keep me
from touching the oven
too long
when it is hot

Life does not always hand us the easy road. Life does not always allow for us to be in the right frame of mind to always do the right thing at the right time. To know this is to remember that you are human. We are not born knowing the best way to navigate the worst circumstances. We are all more than our mistakes. Our mistakes do not make us bad people. Our mistakes, when met with awareness and personal responsibility, are actually what introduce us to our best selves. You are beautiful because of all of your experiences—the good, the bad, and the imperfect. ❦

how to keep going

pause
breathe
repair your universe
proceed

WE ALL REQUIRE HEALING AT
ONE POINT OR ANOTHER. TAKE
TIME TO HEAL YOUR WOUNDS.
TAKE TIME TO HEAL YOUR
HEART. IT DOES NO GOOD
TO THINK ABOUT RUNNING
THE MARATHON WHEN YOU
STILL HAVE A BROKEN FOOT.

MAYBE DON'T DO THINGS

THE WAY YOU HAVE

ALWAYS DONE THEM

SIMPLY BECAUSE THAT

IS THE WAY YOU HAVE

ALWAYS DONE THEM.

cleo wade

There can be no flow without the spirit of flexibility. Allow yourself to be flexible. When we walk into situations feeling so sure of who we are and what we know, we are unable to create space for others or for our own personal growth. When we are flexible, we open ourselves to mountains of possibilities, new ideas, and revelations. To be in flow means to be able to move through the world with the ability to roll with whatever comes up. There is no way to do this if the energy you embody is rigid and stubborn.

Loosen up. ❦

a release

I am holding on
but
my hands are tired
and
turning red
this had me thinking
maybe to love
I had to
let go
instead

Is what you are holding on to taking all of your energy? Are your hands clenched, your body tight, and your soul strained? Whether it is in the realm of your job, your family dynamic, or your romantic relationship, know that just because something is important to us, does not mean we have to control it by attaching stress, worry, and anxiety to it. Let go. Let what is meant to be . . . be. What is meant for us flows freely in harmony with us, not against us. ⋎

REMEMBER NOT TO

CARE ABOUT THE THINGS

YOU DON'T EVEN

CARE ABOUT.

cleo wade

Sometimes our habitual thinking takes over and we end up complaining or being upset about things that don't actually matter to us. Break the habit. Before you get worked up about something, ask yourself, *Do I really value this enough to exhaust myself emotionally over it?* Ask yourself if it is worth it to have it play on a mental loop in your head. Ask yourself if it is worth your energy or worth your words. You are in charge of how much space a thought takes up in your life. Take the time to carefully consider what you let be a part of your being and your spirit. ❧

a message from today

maybe
don't
tomorrow
your
life
away

cleo wade

THE BEST THING ABOUT YOUR
LIFE IS THAT IT IS CONSTANTLY
IN A STATE OF DESIGN.
THIS MEANS YOU HAVE,
AT ALL TIMES, THE POWER TO
REDESIGN IT. MAKE MOVES,
ALLOW SHIFTS, SMILE MORE,
DO MORE, DO LESS, SAY NO,
SAY YES — JUST REMEMBER,
WHEN IT COMES TO YOUR LIFE,
YOU ARE NOT ONLY THE ARTIST
BUT THE MASTERPIECE AS WELL.

IF YOU ARE GRATEFUL FOR WHERE

YOU ARE, YOU HAVE TO RESPECT

THE ROAD THAT GOT YOU THERE.

cleo wade

We must appreciate all that we survive: the small, the medium, and the monumental. Find gratitude in your life story. Wake up every morning and say to yourself, "I made it here from where I started, and I am so proud of that." When we do this, we bless ourselves and feed ourselves with the love required for us to flourish and keep going no matter where we come from or what we have been through. ❦

GENEROSITY NEVER THINKS
PAST THE PRESENT MOMENT.
GENEROSITY IS WHEN
YOU GIVE WHAT YOU CAN GIVE
AND DO WHAT YOU CAN DO
LIKE THERE IS NO TOMORROW.

cleo wade

doing what you can with
what you've got

and even when
I had not a
penny in my pocket
I still knew the joy of giving

I gave my time
I gave my spirit
I gave my heart

I gave myself fully to the moment
and
even through my tears
I gave my smile to the world
(it needed it more than I could have ever imagined)

WHEN WE OVERCOME OUR FEAR OF
FAILING, WE HAVE THE POWER TO
STEP INTO THE MAGNIFICENCE
OF OUR RESILIENCE. DO THE THINGS
YOU ARE AFRAID TO DO.
DO THE THINGS THAT FEEL BIG.
DO THE THINGS THAT SHOW YOU
WHAT YOU ARE MADE OF.

cleo wade

The people we admire for exhibiting excellence are not the people who are perfect or the people who succeed every time. They are the people who recognize that the road to achieving every goal is paved with victory *and* defeat. The triumphant are celebrated not because they win every time but because they never quit when they lose. We are more resilient than we could ever imagine. Keep going. ❦

YOU WANT LOVE?

BE LOVE.

YOU WANT LIGHT?

BE LIGHT.

When you throw a lit match into a fire, the two separate lights never fail to find each other and join as one. This is the same with the energy of love. Love always detects the energy of love, and light never fails to join forces with more light. When we are in a state of positive and loving energy, the whole room feels it; maybe even the whole world feels it. Embody love and light with actions and thoughts that are positive, uplifting, caring, and considerate, and you will find that you attract others who do the same. ❦

YOUR LIFE EXPERIENCES
ARE ONLY AS VALUABLE
AS YOUR ABILITY TO
TURN THEM INTO
LIFE LESSONS.

cleo wade

We cannot always control what happens to us, but we always have the power to leave any situation feeling stronger and wiser than we were before. There is an education waiting for us within all of our experiences, we just have to decide what we do with it. Choose to allow what you go through to fuel your growth rather than stunt it. ❧

BE CAREFUL WHEN IT COMES
TO FOCUSING ON THE OPINIONS
OF OTHERS — YOU COULD END
UP WALKING A DAY IN THE
LIFE OF EVERYONE ELSE'S
SHOES BUT YOUR OWN.

It is a gift in life to have loving friends, family, and

other types of support as sounding boards when

you are in crisis or in need of help or advice, but

remember to balance the opinions of others with your own inner wisdom. No one knows your life the way you do, so while we must always ask for help when we need it and show gratitude for advice from others, we must also know the difference between respectfully considering someone's opinion and giving it the power to dictate our lives. We are here to do things in our own style, make our own mistakes, and learn our own lessons in our own unique way. Do not ignore your intuition. There is an infinite intelligence within you; let it be your guiding light. ❧

CREATE YOUR OWN
FINISH LINES. LET
THERE BE AS MANY
AS YOU WANT, AND
LET THERE BE MANY.

cleo wade

To know that you are a work in progress means to recognize that your goals are also works in progress. A friend of mine once said to me that there is no . . . "there." It reminded me that every single day we are growing into who we will be tomorrow. Because we go through so many stages and phases, it is important to consistently reset our goals so that they can grow with us. When we reset our goals, we allow for each one to flow into the next and connect with all phases of our life. Refresh your goals regularly and with intention. It will help you stay continuously motivated and inspired. ❦

what I lost and what I gained

and then I realized
that to be
more alive
I had to
be
less afraid
so
I did it
I lost my
fear
and gained
my
whole life

ALLOW TODAY TO BE FEARLESS.
WHAT DOES YOUR DAY LOOK LIKE
WITHOUT FEAR? WHAT ARE
THE WORDS YOU ARE HOLDING
BACK BECAUSE OF FEAR?
WHAT ARE THE DREAMS YOU
ARE NOT MAKING INTO
REALITY BECAUSE OF FEAR?
FREE YOURSELF OF THOSE
FEARS. GIVE YOURSELF A
CHANCE TO SEE WHAT YOU
CAN REALLY DO.

AND BE SURE TO KEEP YOUR LIGHT
BRIGHT AND SHINING — YOU NEVER
KNOW JUST HOW MANY PEOPLE
YOU MAY BE A LIGHTHOUSE FOR.
YOU NEVER KNOW HOW MANY
PEOPLE FIND THEIR WAY HOME,
IN EVEN THE WILDEST STORMS,
BECAUSE YOU ARE THERE.

cleo wade

Light is always light no matter the vessel. Do not put pressure on yourself to shine in a specific form. Light can be big, small, loud, or a whisper, but it is always light. Allow your light to take its own shape and shine in its own way. When we embody our own unique light, we have the power to bring healing energy and clarity to any situation. Light allows us to see things for what they are so that we may proceed with understanding, compassion, and grace. We can navigate our journey with much more confidence when we see the world through the light we shine on it. 🙟

what truth will do

and
are we so
scared
that the truth
will hurt us
that we
are willing to
never give it
the opportunity
to
let it
teach us
motivate us
inspire us
heal us
&
maybe
just maybe
free us
too

The best and the worst thing about the truth is that it gets instant results. Do not let fear of what it will reveal keep you from it. Go after it. Let it liberate you. Allow it to give you the gift of clarity so you may move through your life on a more focused and deliberate path. ❧

SOMETIMES THE ONLY THING

ANOTHER PERSON NEEDS IS

FOR US TO BELIEVE IN THEM.

cleo wade

Letting someone know that you believe in them is one of the most fundamental acts of kindness. Be that person for someone. Each person's life is so much more difficult than we could ever imagine. You never know if your words of support could be the sign someone is looking for to feel capable enough to commit to their own greatness. ❦

FIND SOMEONE

BE THEIR ROCK

(KEEP THEM GROUNDED)

BE THEIR NORTH STAR

(HELP THEM FIND THEIR WAY)

LET

THEM

BE THIS

TO YOU

TOO

cleo wade

Create a sacred space for your relationships by attending to them with trust, love, care, kindness, and support. When we set an intention that the energy between ourselves and someone else is a compassionate, judgment-free zone, we make it possible to be loving shelters for one another. Most people in life are just looking for a safe place to be themselves. When we give that to another person and allow them to give that to us as well, it is a way of keeping each other warm even on life's coldest days. ❦

Best friends give loving and sound advice. Best friends cheer for you. Best friends support you as you grow and evolve. Best friends don't let you beat up on yourself. Best friends show you care and compassion. Best friends show up for you not just when you need it most but also in small, thoughtful, day-to-day ways. Most of us are very good at being a best friend to someone else, but what about being one to ourselves? Are we able to reflect inward and give ourselves advice on a troubling situation? Are we able to cheer for ourselves when we take a risk? Are we able to tell ourselves that it is okay when we feel vulnerable as we grow and evolve out of our comfort zones? Are we able to take care of ourselves when stress is ailing our bodies and spirits? Are we able to do the small things that uplift our mood as we go through the day? Learn to become your own best friend. Share yourself with others, but don't forget to give the best of who you are to yourself as well. You are with yourself for as long as you live . . . so it is probably wise to get good at being a best friend to yourself. ❦

owned by you alone

your peace
belongs to you alone
only you
can give it
to yourself
and only you
can take it away

where to find it

kept looking for goodness
kept asking everyone
where I could find the
good in the world
it was not
until I
looked within
and
grew
my own
goodness
that I
began
to see it
everywhere.

PART OF BEING
UNDERSTOOD IS
MAKING YOURSELF
UNDERSTOOD.

Live with intention. Before you do something, ask yourself why. Ask yourself what you want. Ask yourself why you want it. Ask yourself how you want to feel and how you want to live. Investigate. The clarity of knowing what you care about and what motivates you helps you to be better at allowing those things to guide your decision-making. We can often find ourselves where we don't want to be because our goals or sense of self have gotten hijacked by fear-based opportunity-seeking, pressure from others, or our own insecurities. Gift yourself the confidence to be clear about what you want, to be tapped into your driving purpose, and to know the source of your ambitions. Connect to your internal compass; let the integrity of your core values lead you onward and upward. ⚘

*NO ONE WILL EVER BE BETTER AT COMMUNICATING ON YOUR BEHALF THAN YOU. BE HONEST. BE BRAVE. BE CLEAR. BE DIRECT.

YOU DESERVE YOUR DREAMS —

WHO ELSE COULD THEY POSSIBLY

BELONG TO MORE THAN YOU?

Knowing what we deserve gets you one step closer to having it. Every thought, vision, and idea that frequently occurs in our psyche happens for a reason. Our dreams are our destiny's way of communicating with us. We spend far too much of our time looking at our dreams through the veils of the challenges that live between us and our desires. When we approach our dreams with the energy that says "I can, I will, and I am deserving," we are not only much more likely to attain them, we are also able to better enjoy the road that leads us to them. ⚘

REAL LEADERS LEAD WITH LOVE

When we lead with love, we give strength and care to ourselves and others in a way that can transform any situation. It is only the walls of fear, pain, and insecurity that trap us into believing love cannot conquer all. When we work to let down those walls and connect to the DNA of our basic goodness, we are free to lead with love. Those who lead with love live with fairness, empathy, and patience, doing so without conditions, judgment, or discrimination. When we employ those qualities, we are able to navigate even life's most difficult challenges. Lead with love, you will never regret it. ❦

OUR WORK ETHIC

DOES NOT JUST BELONG

AT WORK.

Our work ethic is something that must be applied to our home, our family, our community, and our world. Don't allow for your goals to exist only in the workplace or where they can be financially rewarded. Live with ambition for your entire existence. Every aspect of your life can be made better with your hard work, love, and devotion. ⚘

turn the lock

the past
cannot stay
the past
if
it is always
on your
mind
there is
only one
person
holding the
key
that frees you
from the shackles
of
days gone by

you.

the way out and the way forward

I loved myself
through what I had
been through

this is how

I stayed afloat
even when
life's waters
raised above my head

and when I needed
someone to trust

this is how I knew
which hands
were helping hands
and which

were hurting hands

the only battle

I had been
so focused
on winning
and losing
I did not realize
the only battle
was the one
between me and
myself
for
myself

When we allow for our wins in life to let us feel like we are on top of the world, we give equal power to allowing our losses to make us feel like the weight of the world is on our shoulders. We can enjoy our successes with less ego and more generosity by remembering that our purpose lies in what we bring to the world, not from the accolades the world brings to us. When we focus solely on validations from the outside world, we end up being very easily controlled by circumstance, but when we remain humble and firmly rooted in our ever-present goodness, we can celebrate our accomplishments and learn from our disappointments without letting them be the things that define us. ❧

these things take time

I am
the caterpillar right now
I may not be flying high
like a butterfly
but
I am
sure as hell

grounded

Divine timing is real. The caterpillar enjoys the energy of being grounded as much as it will enjoy the energy of being a butterfly in the sky. This is because one cannot exist without the other, and every phase of the cycle is equally as necessary as the next. You will have less worry in your life when you can appreciate all of the moments of becoming who you are. ❦

DON'T JUST APPRECIATE IT — ENJOY IT.

Complaining is something that seems to come so easy and so naturally to us, but the problem is: complaints have no magic. They don't make anyone's day better, and they don't help any situation. Try going on a complaint cleanse. Monitor when complaints pop into your mind, and instead of saying them out loud, let them go. When we do this, we allow for our language to be part of how we make the world more magical and more peaceful. ❧

YOU ARE MORE OKAY THAN YOU THINK.

as I go forward

I may stumble
but
I stand up
more
than I fall
down

We spend so much of our time focusing on our missteps. When we trip and fall, we seem to only obsess over the ten seconds we were on the ground rather than the rest of our day spent walking perfectly fine. Similarly, in life, we let one heavy moment, month, or year get in the way of our ability to see that we are okay so much more than we are not okay. Falling down does not make us who we are. Standing up does. Rising and continuing to move forward does. ❦

NO ONE'S DAY IS WHAT
YOU THINK IT IS.
BE EXTRA LOVING
IF YOU CAN.

You could be the sign or the inspiration someone

is looking for to know the simplicity of living with

lovingness. Don't keep your sweetness inside of you

or keep it exclusive to your inner circle. Let it be part

of how you move through the world. Be the person

who gives a dollar to someone in need on the street, waves at your neighbor, and smiles at a child walking by. We have all experienced instances in life where a loved one or even a stranger is sharp or harsh with us, and there is a part of us that feels compelled to react with the same energy. But we should ask ourselves: Why affirm negative energy when we can just as easily transform it into positive energy? <u>Be the</u> <u>reason someone realizes how simple it is to be nice.</u> Be someone's muse in that way.

THE SPIRIT IS NEVER HOLDING
US BACK FROM AN
ATTITUDE ADJUSTMENT,
ONLY THE EGO DOES THAT.

cleo wade

With every new day and even every new minute, we have the opportunity to reset our attitude and change our perspective. There will always be people and circumstances that trigger our anger, sadness, or resentment, but when we allow those emotions to stay on a loop in our minds, that is on us, not on them. Instead, if we let go and allow the new day to bring new energy, we are given a clean slate to really understand what is upsetting us and problem-solve from a place of freshness rather than a place of hostility. When we have a better attitude, we create better solutions, and we have a better life. ᗯ

RELEASE JUDGMENT. REPLACE IT
WITH LOVING KINDNESS. RELEASE
PRESSURE REPLACE IT WITH CARE.
RELEASE COMPARISON,
REPLACE IT WITH GRATITUDE.

To reach our most divine potential, we must shed

what does not serve us and exchange it with what does.

Judgment does not feel good. It does not feel good to

be judged, nor does it feel good to judge others. When

we are feeling judged, we often react by responding

with judgment. There are two problems with this strategy. One, when we respond with judgment we lose the ability to peacefully resolve a situation. The other problem with the strategy of responding with judgment when we feel judged is that we lose the ability to access peace of mind. Judgmental thinking is negative thinking, and negative thinking usually triggers more negative thinking. Don't allow judgment to poison your positive thought flow. When our thought life is positive, our mind is calm, optimistic, and ready to powerfully problem-solve. ᴡ

Intimacy requires us to be careful with ourselves. *Full of care.* Intimacy with our thoughts means being careful with them and showing them affection when we have moments of insecurity or doubt, and by expressing our emotions rather than suppressing them. Intimacy with our body means taking care of our body by feeding it with life-affirming food, language, and movement rather than abusing it with shame, holding it to impossible standards, and weighing it down with toxic substances inside it. Intimacy with ourselves means showing up for all aspects of our being and doing it with trust, gentleness, and care. When

we learn how to have intimacy with ourselves, we

are much braver when it comes to creating intimacy

with others.

KNOWING IT WITHIN
HELPS US TO BE
BETTER AT HAVING
IT WITH OTHERS.

with eyes closed

I hold myself tightly and say
I am in this with you
I am here for you
no matter what happens
I will take care of you

doing this
is me
choosing to be on my own team

doing this
is me
learning to hold myself down through even a
hurricane

doing this
is how I am able to
live my life
rather than let
my life
live me

self-intimacy is self-care, self-care is self-love

rooting for each other

do you think
Mother Nature
cares
that any of her
beautiful flowers
grow in an array
of shades and sizes?
or that one grows
in this direction
and one grows in
that direction?
no,
she puts all of them in her
magnificent garden
so they may
be together
and
root
for
each
other

We are here to connect, not compare. There is a reason we are not in this world alone. It is because we are all connected and need each other to function peacefully, purposefully, and powerfully. We cannot know happiness or our true power if we are constantly in a state of comparison and competition. Comparison and extreme competition run on insecurities and the belief in scarcity, which inevitably isolates us from one another. Competition believes there is one pie, and when someone else takes a piece of it there is less for others. Our highest self knows that there is no pie.

Connection rejects the idea of competing for any one thing and runs, instead, on gratitude and abundance, which weave us more deeply into each other's lives so that we may better support each other in the world. Connection knows that everything we accomplish in life is much more fulfilling when we help others along the way. Don't let the spirit of comparison and competition take you somewhere fast, when the the spirit of collaboration can take you some place far instead. ❧

what to do with what we learn

I did not come
into this room
to see the world
through your eyes
I cannot do that
I came here
to listen
not
merely
with my ears
but with
my heart
tell me your
story
and may
I leave
loving more
and knowing better
may I leave here
carrying you in my spirit
as I walk out of
this room
and into
another

No two people are the same, and no two people experience or process a situation the same way. Leave room for the other person's point of view. It matters. Our reality is not the only reality, and it is not wise for us to believe that our reality is the only correct one. We are not here to see things the same way. We are here to share ideas and be in community with each other, and we can only do that by respecting each other's perspectives so that we may cocreate a culture where everyone is better loved and kept safe. ❦

LET LOVE BE THE
ANSWER TO ALL
OF LIFE'S QUESTIONS
(EVEN THE REALLY,
REALLY HARD ONES).

It takes so much bravery to let love be the answer

to all of the questions in our life, especially the dif-

ficult questions during the difficult times, but com-

mitting to that level of courageous tenderness is

exactly what is needed most in the face of adversity. When we decide that we are going to love no matter what, we embody the ability to make peace in a way that can transcend any struggle or conflict. Don't let any situation cause you to create blocks between you and your ability to give love and empathy. Be fearless enough to love without barriers. It is not always easy, but it is always worth it. Let the enduring strength of love carry you through whatever you encounter in life. This is what it means to truly live with compassion. ❧

OUR WISDOM DOES NOT JUST
COME FROM WHAT WE LEARN.
IT ALSO COMES FROM
WHAT WE UNLEARN.

cleo wade

As we go through life, we begin to realize how much our experiences and environments are absorbed into our personality. For example, if we were raised in a home where people yelled when they were angry, then we are very likely to express ourselves the same way when we get angry, or accept that behavior from others. That said, it is never too late to decide to break our habits or change our behavior. When we empower ourselves to unlearn unhealthy behavior, we create more space to learn new and improved ways of being in the world. So whether you do it on your own or with the help of others, unlearn a little. It may teach you more than you could ever imagine. ❦

FEELING COMPLETE

ONLY COMES WITH

THE REALIZATION THAT

WE ARE ALL ONE.

It is so important to recognize that we are all one. You and your children are one. You and your neighbor are one. You and your partner are one. The dangers of the world are furthered only when we decide that the suffering of others is not our problem. Do not live your life in a bubble and, if you do, let it be one that is large enough for all of humanity. Understanding oneness is the first step to understanding inner peace, outer peace, and holistic happiness. ❦

keep shooting for the moon

this may look
like a crash and burn
but it is just
gravity
in its beauty
asking
us to touch down
asking us
to feel the earth we come from
before we reach for the stars
again

cleo wade

tired

I was tired of worrying
so I gave myself my peace back
I was tired of feeling intimidated by what I *should* do
so I pulled up my sleeves
and
got to work on what I *could* do
I was tired of not knowing
so I found out—about myself, my family, my
ancestors, my government, and the struggles of others
I was tired of seeing evil everywhere
so I found the heavenly spots and showed my
neighbors where they
were
I was tired
of looking at the world as one big mess
so I decided to
start cleaning it up
and when people ask me if I am exhausted
I tell them no
because
more than anything
what I got the most tired of
was being tired

Move beyond tolerance. We are not on this planet to tolerate each other. We are here to love each other. We are here to look out for each other. We are here to see each other reach our individual and collective potential. Tolerance is a low-level energy; it has no wings.

UNLIKE TOLERANCE, LOVE LIVES HIGH, IT FLIES, AND HAS THE POWER TO BRING US ALL TO NEW HEIGHTS.

CONFLICT IS INEVITABLE:
ENCOUNTERING CONFLICT
IN OUR LIVES DOES NOT
SAY ANYTHING ABOUT
WHO WE ARE, IT IS OUR
BEHAVIOR IN CONFLICT
THAT SAYS EVERYTHING
ABOUT WHO WE ARE.

Because there is no avoiding conflict in life, it is crucial that we learn to get good at disagreeing with each other. When we remember that not every difference in opinion is an attack, we are able to give the love, the respect, and the compassionate listening required to handle conflict peacefully. Just because someone disagrees with us does not mean that they are against us. Because conflict puts us in such a defensive place, it can trigger anger, frustration, and fear, which often makes us lash out, lose our temper, or shut down. When we realize that there is no such thing as a conflict-free life, we can instead choose to view every conflict as an opportunity to interact with others with a wider heart. Rather than letting conflict prompt behavior that we may not be particularly proud of, let it instead act as a trigger to dive more deeply into lovingkindness. The next time you find yourself in conflict, see it as an opportunity to show the power and bigness of your love. 🌱

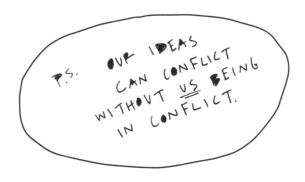

P.S. OUR IDEAS CAN CONFLICT WITHOUT US BEING IN CONFLICT.

DON'T BE THE REASON

SOMEONE

FEELS INSECURE.

BE THE REASON

SOMEONE

FEELS SEEN, HEARD,

AND SUPPORTED

BY THE

ENTIRE UNIVERSE.

cleo wade

The potential for our love to create a macro impact on the world is based on the amount of love we are able to put into our micro connections. Because all of our actions hold energy, everything we do has the power to affect another person. How do you treat others? How do you talk to people? Whether it is your best friend or a stranger, be someone who sees them, who affirms their dignity, and who honors their humanity. Be the person who gives someone the relief of knowing that the world ain't so bad after all. 🌱

HAVE

JOY

Oftentimes when the world feels chaotic, we begin to feel as if it is somehow inappropriate to have joy. Have your joy. Joy is a form of radical self-care. Joy energizes us to take on even the most difficult circumstances. When we have joy, especially in the midst of challenging times, we are saying to the world "I will define the current state of the world around me instead of allowing it to define me." Today, regardless of what is happening, empower yourself by embracing your joy. ⚘

WHEN YOU LOVE WITH

THE SPIRIT OF

ABUNDANCE.

cleo wade

Our words are an extension of our energy. Our words also affirm our energy. If self-love is your struggle, say "I love you" to yourself every single day. It is a way we remind ourselves that we are dedicated to our relationship with ourselves. If you are looking to bring deeper connectivity to your relationships with others, let "I love you" be a declaration you frequently tell the people in your life. It feels good to say I love you. It feels good to let others know that you love them so they don't have to wonder. Affirming our feelings with our words is a way of actively and lovingly investing in the bond we have with ourselves and with everyone else. ❦

THE MOST POWERFUL THING

WE CAN DO WITH WHAT WE

CHOOSE IS TO REGULARLY

RE-CHOOSE IT.

cleo wade

Relationships run on rededication and recommitment. No relationship can sustain itself on one big gesture or one moment of shining behavior. Harmony and stability in our relationships with ourselves, our families, our friends, and our partners come from showing up every single day with a fresh desire for growth, intimacy, and goodness. Love cannot flourish on autopilot. It requires renewed devotion every moment of every day. Devote yourself to love. 🌱

GRATITUDE IS A
CELEBRATION WE
ARE ALL INVITED TO.

I saw a sign in my hometown one day that said, "Until further notice . . . celebrate everything." I have always kept it in my heart as a daily mantra, because it exemplifies the simplicity of gratitude. Oftentimes we think gratitude is this big and complicated idea, but gratitude is simple. It is a thank-you to every-thing and everyone allowing you to be in your story while it unfolds. Our stories may take twists and turns that create barriers between us and our grati-tude, but when we start by finding gratitude in small ways, we will begin to build the momentum we need to find gratitude in big ways. Creating a habit of gratitude also helps us to find it when we need it most. Allow there to be lightness in the journey of finding your gratitude, remembering that it's a party to which you are always invited. ❦

AND REMEMBER — LIFE IS
BIGGER THAN THE BOXES
WE CHECK ALONG THE WAY.

The world is constantly asking us to identify who

we are based on checking a box. We put so much

pressure on ourselves to live within whichever box

we are checking, but the most empowering thing

we could ever do with boxes is design our own. You

are not who you are because of which job, personality type, gender, or race box you check. You are who you are because you are not a box at all, and if you were a box, you would be one that is immense enough to hold all of the boxes that make you feel excited to be alive. So whether it is a writer, cook, accordion player, *New York Times* crossword-puzzle champ, parent, dog-walker, CEO, or lawyer . . . be all of the things. ❦

being and becoming

be who you are
be who you want to be
make those
the same thing
arrive in the world
each day
embracing
yourself

brave enough to show up

yell
if you need to

need
if you need to

live
while you
are here

The world does not need your silence. The world
does not need you to say you
are fine when you aren't.

EXPRESS YOURSELF. DON'T WALK
AROUND WITH THE BURDEN
OF UNSAID THINGS, UNLIVED
TALENTS, AND UNTOLD STORIES.
FREE YOURSELF. LIVE OUT LOUD.

cleo wade

You will never regret standing up for yourself or standing up for someone else. We always have the ability to use our light and our words to protect ourselves and our neighbors from harm. When we allow hurtful or negative behavior to pollute the environment around us, we do a disservice to everyone. No one deserves to be bullied, marginalized, or humiliated by others. Standing up for ourselves and others is something we can always be proud of. Do not allow for darkness to spread because of your silence. Shine light with your voice and your actions instead. ❦

the time has always been now

the time is always right
to begin
the time is always right
to stop waiting on you
the time is always right
to embrace your path
to accept what you had to walk through yesterday
and what you must step away from now as you move toward
tomorrow.
the time is always right
to pound your chest and let them know that you are here.
to let them know that they will hear you
to let them know that they will see you.
the time is always right to
end your silence.
to look at the person next to you and tell them to end their
     silence too
the time is always right to reclaim your narrative
to tell your story
to live with wild freedom
in a place that asks you to
control not only the way you see the world
but also
the way you see yourself
the time is always right to say

I will not be a victim
I will be a survivor
I will be a savior
the time is always right
to remind yourself that you
are going to be okay
the time is always right to love somebody
especially if that somebody is you
the time is always right
to make today
the day
you proclaim that you deserve
your ideas, your dreams, and your hopes
the time is always right
to let waiting
be something
you just don't
do anymore

now is the time,
beloved,
now is the time.

SURROUND YOURSELF

WITH PEOPLE WHO

DESERVE YOUR MAGIC.

cleo wade

One of the chief ways you show yourself love is by surrounding yourself with loving people. When you love yourself, you respect the sacred space you take up in the world. You recognize that no one who sucks your energy, puts you down, makes you feel small, or is unloving to you is entitled to your time. Look around you today and ask yourself if there is anyone in your life that is not showing you the good love you know you know you deserve. ❧

BEING WEIRD IS WHEN YOU
LOVE YOURSELF ENOUGH TO
LIBERATE YOURSELF FROM
THE BURDEN OF TRYING
TO BE NORMAL. IT IS ALSO
WHEN YOU ARE SMART ENOUGH
TO KNOW THAT THERE IS
NO SUCH THING AS NORMAL.

cleo wade

KNOW THAT YOU ARE VALUABLE.

KNOW THAT YOU ARE WORTHY.

KNOW THAT YOU ARE RARE.

HOW COULD ANYONE BE

BETTER THAN YOU IF

YOU ARE THE ONLY YOU?

* SAY THIS TO YOURSELF EVERY SINGLE DAY UNTIL
YOU BELIEVE IT. IT IS TRUE. IT IS REAL. YOU BELONG.

YOU BELONG YOU BELONG YOU BEL

BELONG YOU BELONG YOU BELONG

LONG YOU BELONG YOU BELONG YO

YOU BELONG YOU BELONG YOU BEL

BELONG YOU BELONG YOU BELONG

LONG YOU BELONG YOU BELONG

BELONG YOU BELONG YOU BELO

BELONG YOU BELONG YOU BEL

YOU BELONG YOU BELONG YOU

YOU BELONG YOU BELONG YO

LONG YOU BELONG YOU BELON

YOU BELONG YOU BELONG YOU BE

YOU BELONG YOU BELONG YOU BELO

YOU BELONG YOU BELONG YOU BE

BELONG YOU BELONG YOU BELO

YOU BELONG YOU BELONG YOU
BELONG YOU BELONG YOU BE-
ELONG YOU BELONG YOU BELONG
 YOU BELONG YOU BELONG YOU
BELONG YOU BELONG YOU BE-
BELONG YOU BELONG YOU
YOU BELONG YOU BELONG YOU
 YOU BELONG YOU BELONG
LONG YOU BELONG YOU BELONG
BELONG YOU BELONG YOU BE-
YOU BELONG YOU BELONG
J YOU BELONG YOU BELONG
 YOU BELONG YOU BELONG
J YOU BELONG YOU BELONG YOU
YOU BELONG YOU BELONG YOU BELONG

AND PERHAPS THAT ONE THING
THAT YOU HAVE SPENT YOUR
LIFE WORKING AROUND IS THE
ONE THING YOU ARE MEANT TO
WORK THROUGH INSTEAD.

What are you turning a blind eye to? What aspects of others do you ignore because "it's not even worth it"? What thoughts are you having that you have to talk yourself into feeling are "not that big of a deal"? What are you numbing? There are many circumstances, dynamics, and experiences in our lives that we bribe ourselves to work around, and sometimes that is okay. But it is worth it to ask yourself if any of the things you are working around are keeping you up at night or are things that you are constantly venting about to your friends. If so, change your strategy. Choose to work through what is upsetting you. Dissect it, get to know it, and if you need help, get help. Nothing negative deserves to take up major real estate in your mind or in your heart. ❦

AND WHY NOT MAKE
ALL YOUR TALKS WITH
YOURSELF PEP TALKS?

cleo wade

You are the first person you speak to in the morning. What does that sound like? Are you trash-talking yourself *to* yourself? Are you celebrating yourself? Are you creating a nervous chatter? How you speak to yourself sets the tone for how the rest of the world will speak to you; use that power to lift yourself up and set a standard for loving communication. How you speak to yourself also sets the tone for how you will speak to others. If you learn how to lift yourself up with your words, you will be able to do the same for everyone else. Our world needs more cheerleaders. Start by being one for yourself.

it's all beautiful

why should I
believe in
flaws?

because there is one way that we are all supposed to look?
because someone is selling me something to make me look
more like someone else?

so a company can profit off of not only my money but also my
self-esteem?

because as long as there is a standard of beauty, one type of
person can be celebrated while the rest of us are left out?

wanting, starving, shaming, and hating our beautiful bodies.

why should I
believe in
flaws?

whoever created the concept
does not believe in
me.

let us no longer "embrace our flaws"; we have none. I am me.
you are you.

it's all beautiful.

cleo wade

a love note to my body

a love note to my body:

first of all,
I want to say
thank you.

for the heart you kept beating
even when it was broken

for every answer you gave me in my gut

for loving me back
even when I didn't know how to love you

for every time you recovered when I pushed you past our limits

for today,

for waking up.

FYI: YOU ARE LOVABLE

When you express deep vulnerability or pain, you are still deserving of love. When you are embarrassed, you are still deserving of love. When you are angry, you are still deserving of love. When you need help, you are still deserving of love. When you have to try again, you are still deserving of love. When everything hurts, you are still deserving of love. When you make a mistake, you are still deserving of love. When you cry, you are still deserving of love. Don't let the opinions of others, the "rules" of society, or your own self-shaming uproot you from knowing that you are lovable. When you disconnect with your lovability, you disconnect with your ability to heal. No matter what happens, know that you are always deserving of love. ❦

the day I came home and
turned on the light

to those
who did not treat me well
and, for some reason, wondered why I left:

it is because
I remembered that
I loved myself more
than I loved the idea of
an
"us"

it is because
I remembered
I was worth more
than you could ever
give

it is because
I realized I did not need you

because
I had
me

the day I came home and turned the light on

cleo wade

AND MAY YOUR

FIRST LOVE

LAST FOREVER.

P.S. YOU ARE YOUR FIRST LOVE.

TAKE CARE OF YOURSELF.

getting there

the mind says:
this river has no bottom
the heart says:
we can build a bridge here

I WISH I COULD GIVE YOU
ONE SOLUTION FOR PAIN
THAT DEFINITELY WORKS.
I CAN'T. IT IS A PROCESS
AND IT IS DIFFERENT
FOR EVERYONE, BUT WHAT
I CAN TELL YOU IS THAT
IF YOU ARE BADASS ENOUGH
TO FEEL YOUR PAIN, THEN
YOU ARE BADASS ENOUGH
TO HEAL YOUR PAIN.

LEAN INTO THE TOUGH STUFF.
GROWTH IS NOT ALWAYS
COMFORTABLE. THIS IS WHY
WE CALL THEM GROWING PAINS
NOT GROWING PLEASURES.

cleo wade

Very few breakthroughs come without a few break-downs along the way. Stay the course. Our personal evolution brings so much brilliance to our life, but it can also bring some pain and discomfort with it. While our spiritual and emotional shifts do bring us closer to our best selves, they also simultane-ously move us away from the space in which we may have been comfortably living before. These transi-tional periods, while necessary to our growth, often leave us feeling incredibly vulnerable. Be gentle with yourself. Moving from where you were to where you are takes some getting used to. ❦

HEARTS BREAK.

THAT'S HOW THE MAGIC GETS IN.

Heartbreak is so incredibly mysterious. While on the one hand, we are in so much pain with amplified feelings of loneliness and abandonment, we are also in such an elevated state of sensitivity, allowing us to be hugely in tune to the information our heart has to offer us. When we are in this state of intense intimacy with our heart, we are able to learn so many lessons that benefit our journey and future relationships. We can only fully tap into all that our emotional intelligence has to offer when we are able to really sit with what we are feeling, even when what we are feeling is pain. Try not to avoid pain too much. There is a certain type of magic that comes through pain, for it is where we learn of our power to keep going no matter what we go through. ❦

what happens to pain

time and time again
my soul
and
my spirit
and
my learning heart
prove to me

I heal

it gets better

you will not have the blues forever

forever
is the only thing that lasts forever

when the night sky
falls upon you
look up at her
see the darkness and the vastness
of her blues
hold your eyes steady on her
watch
the sun sneak in
see how even she, the great big sky,
changes with
the new day

this too shall pass

AND MAYBE I HAD BEEN SO

BUSY LOOKING FOR THE PIECES—

I NEVER NOTICED I WAS

ALREADY TOGETHER.

THE WAY YOU LOVE YOURSELF SETS THE
EXAMPLE FOR HOW EVERYONE ELSE
WILL LOVE YOU. SET THE BAR BY
SHOWING YOURSELF RESPECT, LOYALTY,
COMPASSION, KINDNESS, CARE, AND
VULNERABILITY. SHOW US ALL
HOW LOVING YOU IS DONE.

reciprocity

what you want
must be held
in the same
hand
as what
you
give

The energy of reciprocity is what balances our relationships. Healthy reciprocity is not just about giving and receiving, it is about doing those two things well. When we attach exhaustion or resentment to the way we give, then we are not giving in a way that truly helps or benefits anyone involved. Giving should never feel like a negative experience. Equally, when we attach guilt or shame to receiving, we are blocking our ability to receive in a way that truly nourishes us. Our ability to give is only as powerful as our ability to receive, mostly because the more we can know how to receive, the more we have to give. ❦

love is an action verb

I loved back
not because
their love
sounded sweet
but because
their love
had feet
it did not
tell you where
it was going
it showed
you

We can accept only what someone has the ability to give us. When we are able to recognize the difference between someone's *desire* to do something and their *ability* to do something, we are much better at gauging our own expectations and needs from them. Our words often communicate what we *think* we are capable of, while our actions prove what we are *actually* capable of. You will have more clarity in your relationships when you accept the behavior of others based on their actions rather than on their words. ❦

FEAR WORRIES,

"HOW WILL I GET

THERE?"

FAITH SMILES

KNOWINGLY,

"WE WILL GET

THERE."

cleo wade

forgiveness

do not
spend your time
trying to wrap your head
around
the idea of
forgiveness
it is not
intellectual

forgiveness

is spiritual
it is one of the most
spiritual things
we could ever do

Forgive yourself. Forgive yourself for who you were last week, last month, or last year. Forgive yourself for when you were exhausted and snapped at the people you love. Forgive yourself for not being able to do it all. Forgive yourself for your fears. Forgive yourself for your mistakes. Forgive yourself for eating one cookie too many. Forgive yourself for not being perfect. We often look at forgiveness as an intellectual act, but forgiveness is very spiritual. It is one of the most spiritual things we can do. When we forgive, we acknowledge that we are far bigger and greater than one individual

moment. When we forgive, we are saying to the

universe: I will not imprison myself or anyone else

with anger, shame, judgment, or resentment. Gift

yourself this freedom. ❦

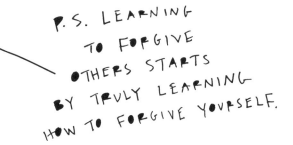

P.S. LEARNING
TO FORGIVE
OTHERS STARTS
BY TRULY LEARNING
HOW TO FORGIVE YOURSELF.

strong flower

baby,
you are
the strongest
flower
that ever
grew
remember that
when
the weather
changes

cleo wade

Know that you are strong. Every living thing on this planet is here with the divine support of Mother Nature. She always has your back. Her type of support system will see you through any weather. The best thing about strength is that when you embody it, you further it, you get stronger. We grow into exactly where we need to be emotionally, spiritually, physically, and intellectually in a way that allows us to handle whatever life has in store for us. Knowing this keeps us inherently prepared so that we can enjoy the sun without worrying about the rain. 🌱

YOU ARE
IN BLOOM.
DID YOU
KNOW THAT?
YOU ARE

IN BLOOM
YOUR WHOLE
LIFE. DID
YOU KNOW
THAT TOO?

I THINK ABOUT
LOVE

(a poem)

I think about love
I wrote on a sheet of paper
one day
love, if you know how.
how to love?
a universe with
no road maps
no gravity
no luxury of polarity
up
feeling so
down

down
feeling
so
down

I think about how
we
want it all
to be
free

and to be
sheltered

to be
the home
and
be *in*
the home
at the same time

I think about
what it means
to be free
in love
to be free
with love

I think about
having the clarity
to know
when to stay
and
when
to go

have we not all
at one point
stayed too long?

cleo wade

I think about
staying too long
it
reminds me
of
past loves

ghosts

as you love
you learn
of ghosts
you are not haunted
by
the person
but
by all
of the ways
you wish
you would have been

the ways
you wish
you knew how
to be

growing up
they do not teach you
all the things
of love

they tell you
love hurts
but
they never tell you
that
there are
some people
there are
some things
you never
get over

I think about
heartbreak
how
hearts break
and
that's how
the magic
gets in

cleo wade

the magic
by the way
does
get in
it never stops
getting
in
but
the other thing
no one tells you
when
you are young
is that
hearts
do not
unbreak
they remain

in pieces
and with
these pieces
you go on
and
you go on

until
one day
you meet
someone
who has pieces too
and together

you
make
a new heart

the other thing
no one tells you
when
you are young
is that
you
meet the person
who
helps you
make
a new heart

and
it is

a gift of
grace and
beauty

beyond imagination

I think about
the gift
of love

how we struggle
to
understand how
to
receive
such a gift

rumi said:
"your task
is not
to seek
for love
but merely
to seek
and find
all of the barriers

within yourself
you have
built up against it"

I think about
how
we should
get to know ourselves
without barriers

I think about
how
we should
get to know ourselves
in a state
that
is not seeking

I think about
how
we are all
chasing
our dreams
meanwhile
our dreams
are

cleo wade

chasing
us

I think about
dreams when
I think about
love
for
one does not exist
without
the other
as
the inhale
is to
the exhale

I think
you should
have good love

I think
you should
have your dreams

I think
those things

belong to you
who else
could they
possibly
belong to
more than you?
and yes
you may
have to
fight for them

that
I know
for sure

and yes
the biggest
battle
may be with
yourself
and
on your own behalf
there is a lot of love
in
our battles

cleo wade

for
to live your life
as a soldier
fighting every day
for
who the hell you are
is
a very strong life

be proud of that

when I think about
being proud

I think about
where
I am from
and
when I say
where
I am from

I mean

a woman

as a girl
I was not sure
how to be

I said things
I did not mean

I said things
I did not
understand

as
a woman
I still have
moments
of being
outside of myself
but
as
a woman
I know now
to ask
what they mean
to
try to understand

cleo wade

to
not only be the help
I need but
to
ask for it
as well

I think about
needing
how
a strange shame
comes
from needing another

how
what's worse
is
the way
we try
to not need
anything from
ourselves

how we
do not ask
what

we need
so
instead
wonder
who
we are

do not
wonder who you are
find out who you are

remembering

that
to decide
to
really and
truly
get to know yourself
is
the bravest
thing
you
could ever do

decide on you

cleo wade

be
the moon
if you want to

be
the lightbulb
in the kitchen
or a flashlight
in the wild

all
I ask
is that
you
shine

for

how to love
can be
a dark universe
with
no signals
where
the lessons
only come

when the past
is
the past
and
you are
sharing your
ghost stories
with
your new heart

but the more
I think about it
the more
I see

that
the clearest route
to bliss
is to
be
alive
while
you
are here
to

be
with yourself
in a
love
so deep
the oceans
get jealous and
even
outer space
wants
to
be inside

that

is
the type
of love
that
shows us all
how

that

is the starting point
from which

to
build
a home
you can invite

the
whole world
into

cleo wade

acknowledgments

I would first like to acknowledge my ancestors and all that came before me. There would be no space in the world for me if they had not first dreamt it and fought for it.

To my brother, Bernardo, who continuously shows me the unbreakable nature of the human spirit and the power within us all to change.

To my mother, Lori, for teaching me what unconditional love and true forgiveness means.

To my father, Bernardo, for teaching me resilience and the art of celebrating life and love.

To my partner, Cory, for being a constant source of light and inspiration in my life. You have truly been my rock during this process. Thank you, ML.

To Jewels Rosaasen for keeping me sane; I treasure you beyond words.

To Jenna Barclay, who spent countless hours workshopping this book with me. I am eternally grateful for the many ways you have nurtured my spiritual journey over the years.

To Heather Karpas for your passion, incredible friendship, and dedication to this book.

To Dawn Davis, Dana Sloan, Trisha Tan, Albert Tang, and the entire team at 37 INK, this book would not be possible without your hard work. Thank you one million times.

A special thank-you to all of the Goddesses, Queens, Soul Sisters, and Angels in my life. You are my muses, my support system, and my family. I would not be the woman I am without the love, magic, and friendship we share.

These pages have been inspired by many friends and mentors along the way. Thank you all for your advice and wisdom.

And to everyone who has supported my work over the years, thank you for being my a part of my family. You mean the world to me.

Love,
Cleo